O9-AIG-284

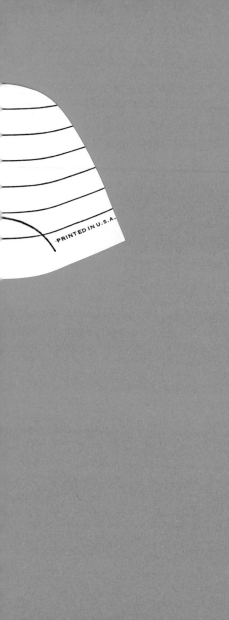

DAILY
PEACE

DAILY
PEACE

365
DAYS OF
RENEWAL

Photos and Wisdom to Nourish Your Spirit

NATIONAL
GEOGRAPHIC

WASHINGTON, D.C.

Since 1888, the National Geographic Society has funded more than 12,000 research, exploration, and preservation projects around the world. National Geographic Partners distributes a portion of the funds it receives from your purchase to National Geographic Society to support programs including the conservation of animals and their habitats.

National Geographic Partners
1145 17th Street NW
Washington, DC 20036-4688 USA

Get closer to National Geographic explorers and photographers, and connect with our global community. Join us today at nationalgeographic.com/join

For information about special discounts for bulk purchases, please contact National Geographic Books Special Sales: specialsales@natgeo.com

For rights or permissions inquiries, please contact National Geographic Books Subsidiary Rights: bookrights@natgeo.com

Library of Congress Cataloging-in-Publication Data
Daily peace : 365 days of renewal : photos and wisdom to nourish your spirit.
pages cm
Includes index.
ISBN 978-1-4262-1565-0 (hardcover : alk. paper)
1. Meditations. 2. Spiritual life. 3. Devotional calendars. 4. Photography, Artistic.
BL624.2.D33 2015
158.1'28--dc23

2014050009

Interior design by Katie Olsen

Printed in China

18/PPS/2

JANUARY
TRANSITION

There are far, far better things ahead
than any we leave behind.

~ C. S. LEWIS

JANUARY 2

True progress quietly and persistently
moves along without notice.

~ St. Francis de Sales

There is a joy
in the pursuit of anything.

~ ROBERT HENRI

JANUARY 4

We must be willing to get rid
of the life we've planned, so as to have
the life that is waiting for us.

~ JOSEPH CAMPBELL

Progress is impossible
without change;
and those who cannot
change their minds
cannot change anything.

~ GEORGE BERNARD SHAW

JANUARY 6

What saves a man is to take a step.
Then another step. It is always the same step,
but you have to take it.

~ ANTOINE DE SAINT-EXUPÉRY

Time is the greatest innovator.

~ FRANCIS BACON

Wherever we are, it is but a stage on the way
to somewhere else, and whatever we do,
however well we do it, it is only a preparation
to do something else that shall be different.

~ ROBERT LOUIS STEVENSON

We must always change, renew,
rejuvenate ourselves so that we don't
become stick-in-the-muds.

~ GOETHE

JANUARY 10

In the midst of chaos,
there is also opportunity.

~ SUN TZU

JANUARY 11

If there were none who were discontented
with what they have, the world would
never reach for anything better.

~ FLORENCE NIGHTINGALE

We spend our lives avoiding the situations
that help us grow. It's when we stay
with uncertainty and discomfort
without trying to fix it that we connect
with our own innate joy, wisdom, and love.

~ PEMA CHÖDRÖN

Don't be too timid and squeamish
about your actions.
All life is an experiment.
The more experiments you make
the better.

~ RALPH WALDO EMERSON

JANUARY 14

I have always known that
at last I would take this road,
but yesterday I did not know
that it would be today.

~ NARIHIRA

JANUARY 15

Pursue some path, however narrow
and crooked, in which you can walk
with love and reverence.

~ HENRY DAVID THOREAU

These are the days
that must happen to you.

~ WALT WHITMAN

JANUARY 17

If you want to succeed you should
strike out on new paths, rather than travel
the worn paths of accepted success.

~ JOHN ROCKEFELLER

JANUARY 18

Every great change
is preceded by chaos.

~ DEEPAK CHOPRA

Tomorrow belongs to those
who can hear it coming.

~ DAVID BOWIE

First say to yourself what you would be;
and then do what you have to do.

~ EPICTETUS

JANUARY 21

It's no use going back to yesterday,
because I was a different person then.

~ LEWIS CARROLL

Many things which
cannot be overcome
when they are together,
yield themselves up
when taken little by little.

~ PLUTARCH

You are never too old to set another goal
or to dream a new dream.

~ C. S. LEWIS

JANUARY 24

There is no reason
not to follow your heart.

~ STEVE JOBS

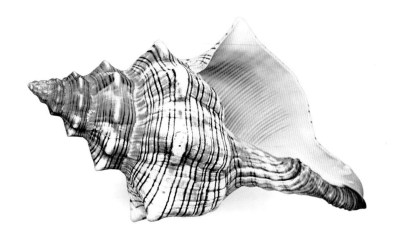

Growth and self-transformation
cannot be delegated.

~ LEWIS MUMFORD

There is no real development
without integrity,
that is—a love of truth.

~ FRANK LLOYD WRIGHT

JANUARY 27

No one saves us
but ourselves.
No one can and
no one may.
We ourselves
must walk the path.

~ BUDDHA

Things which do not grow
and change are dead things.

~ LOUISE ERDRICH

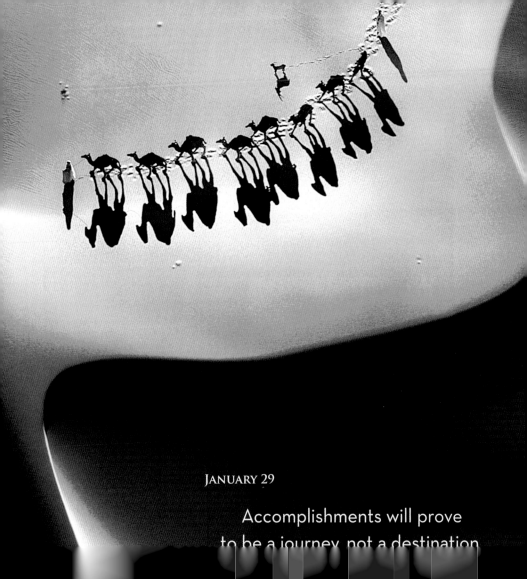

JANUARY 29

Accomplishments will prove
to be a journey, not a destination

JANUARY 30

It's good to have an end
to journey toward; but it's the journey
that matters in the end.

~ URSULA K. LE GUIN

In order to be who you are,
you must be willing to let go
of who you think you are.

~ MICHAEL SINGER

FEBRUARY

HEALING

What is required of us is that we love
the difficult and learn to deal with it.
In the difficult are the friendly forces,
the hands that work on us.

~ RAINER MARIA RILKE

The love of the family,
the love of the person can heal.
It heals the scars left by a larger society.
A massive, powerful society.

~ MAYA ANGELOU

FEBRUARY 3

To be alive at all
is to have scars.

~ JOHN STEINBECK

FEBRUARY 4

Your problem is you
are too busy holding on
to your unworthiness.

~ RAM DASS

Be patient and tough;
someday this pain
will be useful to you.

~ OVID

When you learn your lessons,
the pain goes away.

~ ELISABETH KÜBLER-ROSS

Find meaning.
Distinguish melancholy
from sadness.
Go out for a walk.

~ ALBERT CAMUS

It is the nature of grace to fill
the places that have been empty.

~ GOETHE

Everybody talks about wanting
to change things and help and fix—
but ultimately all you can do is fix yourself.
Because if you can fix yourself,
it has a ripple effect.

~ ROB REINER

The best remedy for those who are afraid, lonely or unhappy is to go outside, somewhere where they can be quiet, alone with the heavens, nature and God. Because only then does one feel that all is as it should be.

~ ANNE FRANK

Sorrow fully accepted brings its own gifts.
For there is alchemy in sorrow.
It can be transmuted into wisdom,
which, if it does not bring joy,
can yet bring happiness.

~ PEARL S. BUCK

Forgive your anger. Forgive your guilt.
Your shame. Your sadness. Embrace and
open up your love, your joy, your truth,
and most especially your heart.

~ JIM HENSON

When the heart is right,
the mind and body will follow.

~ CORETTA SCOTT KING

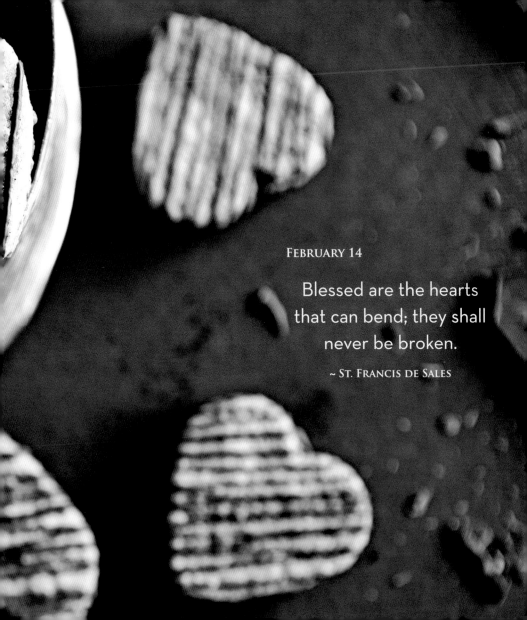

FEBRUARY 14

Blessed are the hearts
that can bend; they shall
never be broken.

~ St. Francis de Sales

The truth will set you free.
But not until it is finished with you.

~ DAVID FOSTER WALLACE

I will not say, do not weep,
for not all tears are an evil.

~ J.R.R. TOLKIEN

You cannot find peace by avoiding life.

~ SIR DAVID HARE

If better were within,
better would come out.

~ SIMON PATRICK

Someday you're gonna
look back on this moment
of your life as such
a sweet time of grieving.
You'll see that you were in
mourning and your heart
was broken, but your life
was changing.

~ ELIZABETH GILBERT

Crying is all right in its way while it lasts.
But you have to stop sooner or later,
and then you still have to decide what to do.

~ C. S. LEWIS

FEBRUARY 21

Perhaps somewhere,
someplace deep inside your being,
you have undergone important
changes while you were sad.

~ RAINER MARIA RILKE

FEBRUARY 22

If there is to be any peace it will come
through being, not having.

~ HENRY MILLER

The deeper that sorrow
carves into your being,
the more joy you can contain.

~ KAHLIL GIBRAN

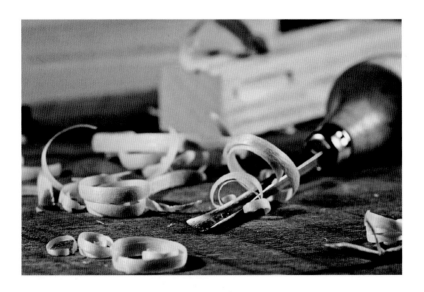

FEBRUARY 24

We are healed
of a suffering only
by experiencing it
to the full.

~ MARCEL PROUST

FEBRUARY 25

The wound is the place
where light enters you.

~ RUMI

What we achieve inwardly
will change outer reality.

~ PLUTARCH

… Be gentle with yourself. You are a child
of the universe, no less than the trees
and the stars; you have a right to be here.

~ MAX EHRMANN

What happens when
people open their hearts?
They get better.

~ HARUKI MURAKAMI

MARCH

RESILIENCE

March 1

Our business in this world is not to succeed,
but to continue to fail, in good spirits.

~ Robert Louis Stevenson

Never underestimate the power of dreams
and the influence of the human spirit.
The potential for greatness
lives within each of us.

~ WILMA RUDOLPH

MARCH 3

If you can learn from hard knocks,
you can also learn from soft touches.

~ CAROLYN KENMORE

Nothing will work unless you do.

~ MAYA ANGELOU

You build on failure.
You use it as a stepping-stone.
Close the door on the past.

~ JOHNNY CASH

Dearly beloved,
we are gathered here today
to get through this thing called life.

~ PRINCE

You have to pick
the places you don't
walk away from.

~ JOAN DIDION

MARCH 8

The secret of life
is to fall seven times
and to get up eight times.

~ PAULO COELHO

You mustn't confuse a single failure
with a final defeat.

~ F. SCOTT FITZGERALD

Have patience with all things
but first with yourself.
Never confuse your mistakes
with your value as a human being.

~ St. Francis de Sales

The first great rule of life
is to put up with things.

~ BALTASAR GRACIÁN

MARCH 12

What lies behind us and
what lies before us
are tiny matters
compared to what
lies within us.

~ HENRY STANLEY HASKINS

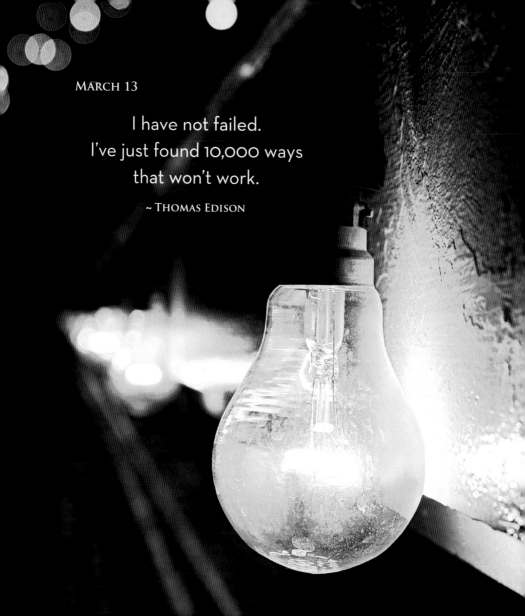

MARCH 13

I have not failed.
I've just found 10,000 ways
that won't work.

~ THOMAS EDISON

MARCH 14

Once the storm is over, you won't remember
how you made it through, how you managed
to survive. You won't even be sure whether
the storm is really over. But one thing is certain:
When you come out of the storm, you won't
be the same person who walked in.
That's what this storm's all about.

~ HARUKI MURAKAMI

Hardships often prepare
ordinary people
for extraordinary destiny.

~ C. S. LEWIS

You may not control all the events
that happen to you, but you can decide
not to be reduced by them.

~ MAYA ANGELOU

There are some things
you learn best in calm,
and some in storm.

~ WILLA CATHER

MARCH 18

Start by doing what's necessary,
then what's possible, and suddenly
you are doing the impossible.

~ St. Francis of Assisi

The most beautiful people we have known
are those who have known defeat,
known suffering, known struggle, known loss,
and have found their way out of the depths.
These persons have an understanding of life
that fills them with compassion,
gentleness, and a deep loving concern.
Beautiful people do not just happen.

~ ELISABETH KÜBLER-ROSS

It is impossible to live without
failing at something, unless you live
so cautiously that you might as well not
have lived at all—in which case,
you fail by default.

~ J. K. ROWLING

MARCH 21

Out of suffering have emerged
the strongest souls; the most massive
characters are seared with scars.

~ KAHLIL GIBRAN

It is not the strongest
or the most intelligent
who will survive,
but those who can
best manage change.

~ CHARLES DARWIN

To be fully human is to know
that it's possible to face the
unimaginable and somehow
put one foot in front of the other.

~ OPRAH WINFREY

Hope begins in the dark, the stubborn hope
that if you just show up and try to do
the right thing, the dawn will come.
You want and watch and work; you don't give up.

~ ANNE LAMOTT

Part of being optimistic
is keeping one's head
pointed toward the sun,
one's feet moving forward.

~ NELSON MANDELA

MARCH 26

Finish each day and be done with it.
You have done what you could. Some blunders
and absurdities no doubt crept in; forget them
as soon as you can. Tomorrow is a new day.
You shall begin it serenely and with too high a spirit
to be encumbered with your old nonsense.

~ Ralph Waldo Emerson

There was never
a night or a problem
that could defeat
sunrise or hope.

~ SIR BERNARD WILLIAMS

Surely, in the light of history,
it is more intelligent to hope rather
than to fear, to try rather than not to try.
For one thing we know beyond all doubt:
Nothing has ever been achieved
by the person who says, "It can't be done."

~ ELEANOR ROOSEVELT

The promised land always lies on
the other side of the wilderness.

~ HAVELOCK ELLIS

MARCH 30

We shall draw from the heart
of suffering itself the means
of inspiration and survival.

~ WINSTON CHURCHILL

The first and final thing you have
to do in this world is to last it
and not be smashed by it.

~ ERNEST HEMINGWAY

APRIL

STRENGTH

APRIL 1

Be truthful, gentle,
and fearless.

~ MAHATMA GANDHI

You have power over your mind—
not outside events. Realize this
and you will find strength.

~ MARCUS AURELIUS

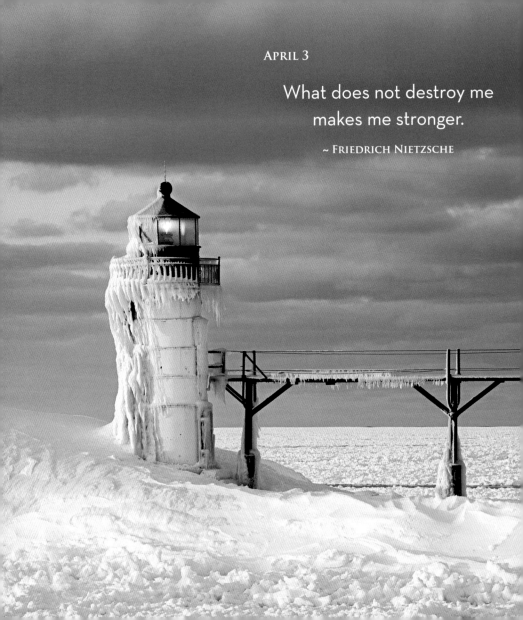

APRIL 3

What does not destroy me
makes me stronger.

~ FRIEDRICH NIETZSCHE

APRIL 4

You can, you should—and if you're
brave enough to start, you will.

~ STEPHEN KING

If you dare nothing,
then when the day is over,
nothing is all you have gained.

~ NEIL GAIMAN

Always go too far, because that's
where you'll find the truth.

~ ALBERT CAMUS

April 7

Great people do things
before they're ready.
They do things before
they know they can do it.

~ Amy Poehler

APRIL 8

Greatness lies not in being strong,
but in the right use of strength.

~ HENRY WARD BEECHER

Tenderness and kindness are not
signs of weakness and despair,
but manifestations of strength
and resolution.

~ Kahlil Gibran

Let me not pray to be sheltered from dangers
but to be fearless in facing them.
Let me not beg for the stilling of my pain,
but for the heart to conquer it.

~ RABINDRANATH TAGORE

I read and walked for miles at night
along the beach, writing bad blank verse
and searching endlessly for someone wonderful
who would step out of the darkness
and change my life. It never crossed my mind
that that person could be me.

~ ANNA QUINDLEN

APRIL 12

Face your life, its pain, its pleasure.
Leave no path untaken.

~ NEIL GAIMAN

So many of our dreams at first seem
impossible, then they seem improbable,
and then, when we summon the will,
they soon become inevitable.

~ CHRISTOPHER REEVE

APRIL 14

When the whole world is silent,
even one voice becomes powerful.

~ MALALA YOUSAFZAI

APRIL 15

To live we must conquer incessantly;
we must have the courage to be happy.

~ Henri-Frédéric Amiel

If you make a choice that goes
against what everyone else thinks,
the world doesn't fall apart.

~ OPRAH WINFREY

Freedom lies in being bold.

~ ROBERT FROST

APRIL 18

We do not need magic to change
the world. We carry all the power we need
inside ourselves already; we have
the power to imagine better.

~ J. K. ROWLING

In the long run,
the sharpest weapon
of all is a kind
and gentle spirit.

~ ANNE FRANK

True courage is not only a balloon for rising
but also a parachute for falling.

~ KARL LUDWIG BÖRNE

APRIL 21

Some of us think holding on makes us strong—
but sometimes it is letting go.

~ HERMANN HESSE

APRIL 22

Nothing but courage can guide life.

~ Vauvenargues

APRIL 23

Faith can give us the courage
to face the uncertainties
of the future.

~ MARTIN LUTHER KING, JR.

Courage is rightly esteemed the first
of human qualities because it is
the quality which guarantees all others.

~ WINSTON CHURCHILL

APRIL 25

Labor to keep alive in your breast
that little spark of celestial fire
called conscience.

~ GEORGE WASHINGTON

APRIL 26

Promise me
you'll always remember:
You're braver than
you believe, and stronger
than you seem, and
smarter than you think.

~ A. A. MILNE

If you aren't in over your head,
how do you know how tall you are?

~ T. S. ELIOT

APRIL 28

Just a step at a time—meeting each thing
that comes up, seeing it is not as dreadful
as it appeared, discovering we have
the strength to stare it down.

~ ELEANOR ROOSEVELT

You were born with potential. You were born
with goodness and trust. You were born with ideals
and dreams. You were born with greatness. You were born
with wings. You are not meant for crawling, so don't.
You have wings. Learn to use them and fly.

~ RUMI

There is nothing the body suffers
that the soul may not profit by.

~ GEORGE MEREDITH

MAY
ACCEPTANCE

If you realize that you have enough,
you are truly rich.

~ LAO-TZU

MAY 2

Whatever the present moment contains,
accept it as if you had chosen it.

~ ECKHART TOLLE

MAY 3

Be yourself.
Everyone else is taken.

~ OSCAR WILDE

MAY 4

Accept who you are;
and revel in it.

~ MITCH ALBOM

MAY 5

You have to accept
whatever comes and
the only important thing
is that you meet it
with the best you
have to give.

~ ELEANOR ROOSEVELT

Connection is the energy that exists between people when they feel seen, heard, and valued; when they can give and receive without judgment; and when they derive sustenance and strength from the relationship.

~ BRENÉ BROWN

Accept the things to which fate binds you,
and love the people with whom fate brings
you together—but do so with all your heart.

~ MARCUS AURELIUS

For all that has been, thanks.
For all that will be, yes.

~ DAG HAMMARSKJÖLD

MAY 9

Peace comes from within.
Do not seek it without.

~ BUDDHA

MAY 10

You is kind.
You is smart.
You is important.

~ KATHRYN STOCKETT

MAY 11

Be kind—for everyone you meet
is fighting a hard battle.

~ PLATO

Let us not fear the hidden.
Or each other.

~ MURIEL RUKEYSER

You are built not to shrink down
to less, but to blossom into more.
To be more splendid. To be more extraordinary.
To use every moment to fill yourself up.

~ OPRAH WINFREY

MAY 14

Accept no one's definition
of your life; define yourself.

~ HARVEY FIERSTEIN

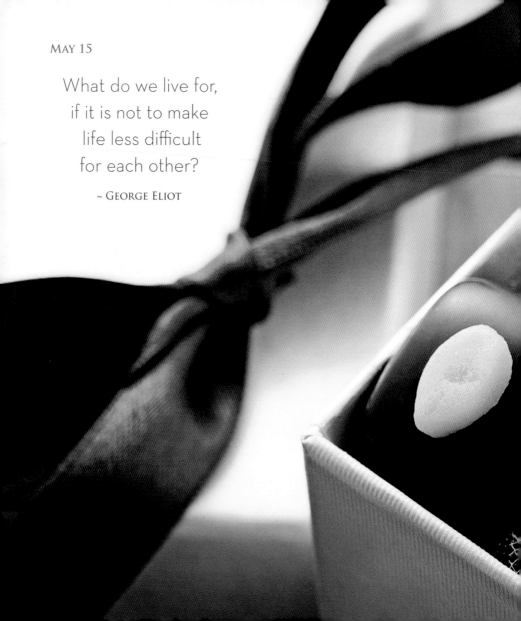

MAY 15

What do we live for,
if it is not to make
life less difficult
for each other?

~ GEORGE ELIOT

To have that sense of one's intrinsic worth . . .
is potentially to have everything.

~ JOAN DIDION

MAY 17

Perfection is the willingness
to be imperfect.

~ LAO-TZU

MAY 18

There is within each one of us a potential
for goodness beyond our imagining; for giving
which seeks no reward; for listening
without judgment; for loving unconditionally.

~ DAVID KESSLER

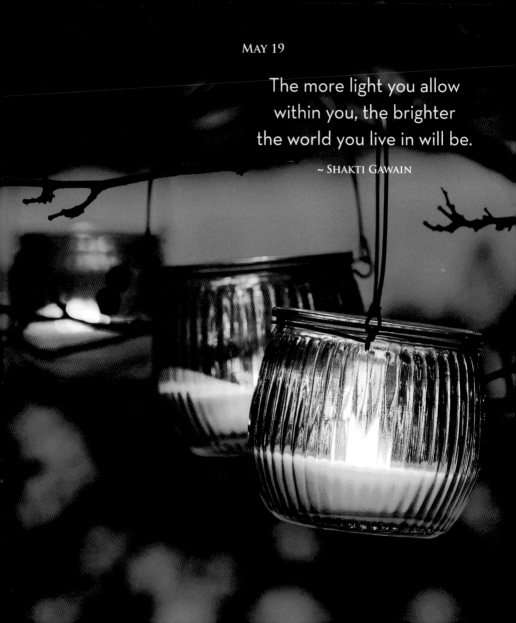

MAY 19

The more light you allow
within you, the brighter
the world you live in will be.

~ SHAKTI GAWAIN

MAY 20

We travel, some of us
forever, to seek other
states, other lives,
other souls.

~ ANAÏS NIN

May 21

MAY 21

We accept the love
we think we deserve.

~ STEPHEN CHBOSKY

The worst loneliness is to not
be comfortable with yourself.

~ MARK TWAIN

MAY 23

Say not, "I have found the truth,"
but rather, "I have found a truth."

~ KAHLIL GIBRAN

You yourself, as much as anybody
in the entire universe,
deserve your love and affection.

~ Buddha

Change is one thing.
Acceptance is another.

~ ARUNDHATI ROY

When we love a person, we accept him
or her exactly as is: the lovely with the unlovely,
the strong with the fearful, the true mixed
in with the façade. And of course, the only way
we can do it is by accepting ourselves that way.

~ MR. ROGERS

Whatever happens to you belongs to you.
Make it yours. Feed it to yourself
even if it feels impossible to swallow.
Let it nurture you, because it will.

~ CHERYL STRAYED

MAY 28

There was another life
that I might have had,
but I am having this one.

~ KAZUO ISHIGURO

MAY 29

You are your best thing.

~ TONI MORRISON

Where the myth fails,
human love begins.
Then we love a human being;
not our dream,
but a human being with flaws.

~ ANAÏS NIN

You don't need to be
accepted by others.
You need to accept yourself.

~ THÍCH NHAT HANH

JUNE
FORGIVENESS

When you forgive,
you love.

~ JON KRAKAUER

We can never obtain peace
in the outer world until
we make peace with ourselves.

~ DALAI LAMA XIV

You will come to know things
that can only be known with the
wisdom of age and the grace of years.
Most of those things will have
to do with forgiveness.

~ CHERYL STRAYED

JUNE 4

Forgiveness is not
an occasional act,
it is a constant attitude.

~ MARTIN LUTHER KING, JR.

JUNE 5

It's simple: When you
haven't forgiven those
who've hurt you,
you turn your back
against your future.
When you do forgive,
you start walking forward.

~ TYLER PERRY

JUNE 6

Forgiving is not forgetting; it's actually remembering—
remembering and not using your right to hit back.
It's a second chance for a new beginning.
And the remembering part is particularly important.
Especially if you don't want to repeat what happened.

~ DESMOND TUTU

We can't go back.
We can only go forward.

~ LIBBA BRAY

JUNE 8

Until we have seen someone's darkness,
we don't really know who that person is.
Until we have forgiven someone's darkness,
we don't really know what love is.

- MARIANNE WILLIAMSON

Everything is just as it needs to be.
And if we would forgive, our minds
and hearts would open and
we could see another possibility.

~ IYANLA VANZANT

It's one of the
greatest gifts
you can give yourself,
to forgive.
Forgive everybody.

~ MAYA ANGELOU

We say of some things that
they can't be forgiven, or that
we will never forgive ourselves.
But we do—we do it all the time.

~ ALICE MUNRO

JUNE 12

The only way out of the labyrinth
of suffering is to forgive.

~ JOHN GREEN

JUNE 13

If we learn to open our hearts,
anyone, including the people
who drive us crazy, can be our teacher.

~ Pema Chödrön

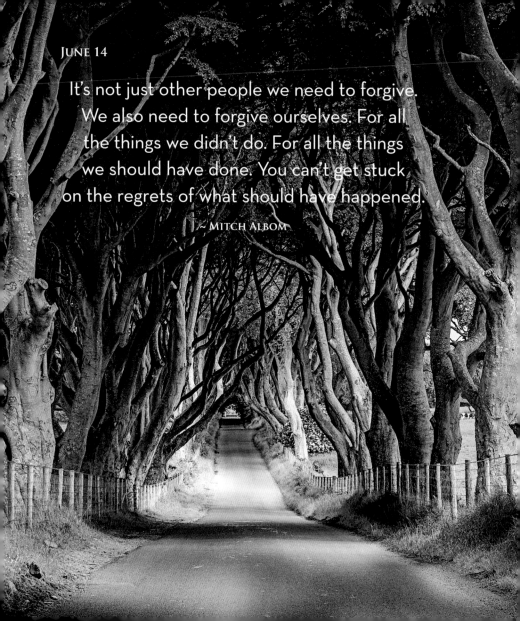

JUNE 14

It's not just other people we need to forgive.
We also need to forgive ourselves. For all
the things we didn't do. For all the things
we should have done. You can't get stuck
on the regrets of what should have happened.

~ MITCH ALBOM

JUNE 15

We must be saved by
the final form of love,
which is forgiveness.

~ Reinhold Niebuhr

What I cannot love,
I overlook.

~ ANAÏS NIN

Those who have the largest hearts
have the soundest understandings.

~ WILLIAM HAZLITT

JUNE 18

Hanging on to resentment
is letting someone you despise
live rent-free in your head.

~ ANN LANDERS

To be wronged is nothing,
unless you continue
to remember it.

~ CONFUCIUS

JUNE 20

The practice of forgiveness
is our most important contribution
to the healing of the world.

~ MARIANNE WILLIAMSON

JUNE 21

If your compassion
does not include yourself,
it is incomplete.

~ BUDDHA

JUNE 22

We need the courage to learn
from our past and not live in it.

~ SHARON SALZBERG

We should be rigorous
in judging ourselves and
gracious in judging others.

~ JOHN WESLEY

Forgiveness is a virtue
of the brave.

~ INDIRA GANDHI

JUNE 25

It is not enough
to know that love
and forgiveness are
possible. We have
to find ways to
bring them to life.

~ JACK KORNFIELD

It is compassion,
the most gracious of virtues,
which moves the world.

~ THIRUVALLUVAR

Charity means pardoning what is
unpardonable, or it is no virtue at all.
Hope means hoping when things
are hopeless, or it is no virtue at all.
And faith means believing in the incredible,
or it is no virtue at all.

~ G. K. CHESTERTON

JUNE 28

Forgiveness is an act of the will,
and the will can function regardless
of the temperature of the heart.

~ CORRIE TEN BOOM

When you forgive somebody—
when you are generous, when you
withhold judgment, when you love
and when you stand up to injustice—
you are, in that moment,
bringing heaven to earth.

.~ ROB BELL

Forgiveness is the act
of admitting we
are like other people.

~ CHRISTINA BALDWIN

JULY

MINDFULNESS

Forever is composed of nows.

~ EMILY DICKINSON

JULY 2

Remember that wherever your heart is,
there you will find your treasure.

~ PAULO COELHO

The only way to live is
by accepting each minute as
an unrepeatable miracle.

~ STORM JAMESON

JULY 4

Some things are
more precious because
they don't last long.

~ OSCAR WILDE

JULY 5

Please notice when you are happy—
and exclaim or murmur or think
at some point, "If this isn't nice,
I don't know what is."

~ KURT VONNEGUT

Be at least as interested in what
goes on inside you as what happens
outside. If you get the inside right,
the outside will fall into place.

~ ECKHART TOLLE

JULY 7

We can only be said
to be alive in
those moments
when our hearts
are conscious
of our treasures.

~ THORNTON WILDER

Try to learn to breathe deeply,
really to taste food when you eat, and when
you sleep to really sleep. When you laugh,
laugh like hell. And when you get angry,
get good and angry. Try to be alive.

~ WILLIAM SAROYAN

For things to reveal themselves to us,
we need to be ready to abandon
our views about them.

~ THÍCH NHAT HANH

Words are timeless. You should utter
them or write them with a knowledge
of their timelessness.

- KHALIL GIBRAN

JULY 11

That it will never come again
is what makes life so sweet.

~ EMILY DICKINSON

JULY 12

Happiness rarely is
absent; it is we that
know not
of its presence.

~ MAURICE MAETERLINCK

JULY 13

Every word has consequences.
Every silence, too.

~ JEAN-PAUL SARTRE

The butterfly counts
not months but moments,
and has time enough.

~ RABINDRANATH TAGORE

JULY 15

If you correct your mind,
the rest of your life will fall into place.

~ LAO-TZU

JULY 16

Thought is invisible nature,
nature is visible thought.

~ HEINRICH HEINE

Always be on the watch
for the coming of wonders.

~ E. B. WHITE

JULY 18

Not in another place but this place,
not for another hour but this hour.

~ WALT WHITMAN

It isn't what we say or think
that defines us, but what we do.

~ JANE AUSTEN

If we could see the miracle
of a single flower clearly,
our whole life would change.

~ BUDDHA

JULY 21

We are what we pretend to be,
so we must be careful
what we pretend to be.

~ KURT VONNEGUT

Look closely at the
present you are
constructing. It should
look like the future
you are dreaming.

~ ALICE WALKER

JULY 23

How noble and good everyone could be if,
every evening before falling asleep, they were
to recall to their minds the events of the whole day
and consider exactly what has been good and bad.
Then without realizing it, you try to improve yourself
at the start of each new day.

~ ANNE FRANK

The aim of life is to live, and to live
means to be aware—joyously, drunkenly,
serenely, divinely aware.

~ HENRY MILLER

All that we are is the result
of what we have thought.

~ BUDDHA

JULY 26

The true way to live is to enjoy
every moment as it passes—and surely
it is in the everyday things around us
that the beauty of life lies.

~ LAURA INGALLS WILDER

JULY 27

The universe is full
of magical things
patiently waiting
for our wits
to grow sharper.

~ EDEN PHILLPOTTS

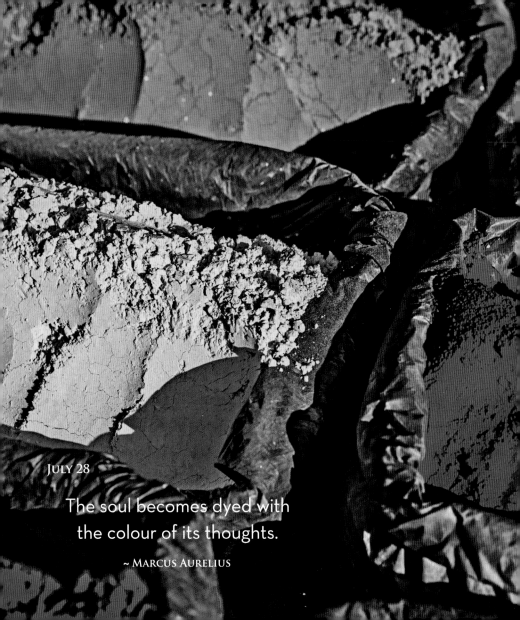

JULY 28

The soul becomes dyed with
the colour of its thoughts.

~ MARCUS AURELIUS

To forget one's purpose
is the commonest form of stupidity.

~ FRIEDRICH NIETZSCHE

Often in life, the most important
question we can ask ourselves is:
do we really have the problem
we think we have?

~ SHERI FINK

JULY 31

The very least you can do in your life
is figure out what you hope for.
And the most you can do is live inside
that hope. Not admire it from a distance,
but live right in it, under its roof.

~ BARBARA KINGSOLVER

AUGUST

PERSPECTIVE

AUGUST 1

Shut your eyes and see.

~ JAMES JOYCE

What you see and hear depends
a good deal on where you are standing:
it also depends on what sort
of person you are.

~ C. S. LEWIS

Write it on your heart
that every day is
the best day in the year.

~ RALPH WALDO EMERSON

The tree which moves some
to tears of joy is in the eyes
of others only a green thing
that stands in the way.

~ WILLIAM BLAKE

If the only prayer you ever say
in your whole life is "thank you,"
that would suffice.

~ MEISTER ECKHART

The universe is true for all of us
and different for each of us.

~ MARCEL PROUST

AUGUST 7

We shall see but a little
way if we require to
understand what we see.

~ Henry David Thoreau

AUGUST 8

Most problems, if you give them
enough time and space, will eventually
wear themselves out.

~ BUDDHA

Only if you have been in
the deepest valley can you ever know
how magnificent it is to be
on the highest mountain.

~ RICHARD M. NIXON

We can always choose
to perceive things differently.
We can focus on what's wrong in our life,
or we can focus on what's right.

~ MARIANNE WILLIAMSON

What you believe has more power
than what you dream or wish or hope for.
You become what you believe.

~ OPRAH WINFREY

The quieter you become,
the more you can hear.

~ RAM DASS

AUGUST 13

There is no such thing in anyone's life
as an unimportant day.

~ ALEXANDER WOOLLCOTT

Be glad of life because it gives you
the chance to love and to play
and to look at the stars.

~ HENRY VAN DYKE

If you look the right way, you can see
that the whole world is a garden.

~ FRANCES HODGSON BURNETT

AUGUST 16

We see with our eyes.
We know with our hearts.

~ JIM HENSON

AUGUST 17

The longest journey
is the journey inward.

~ DAG HAMMARSKJÖLD

Miracles are a retelling in small letters
of the very same story which is written
across the whole world in letters
too large for some of us to see.

~ C. S. LEWIS

What the caterpillar calls
the end, the rest of the world
calls a butterfly.

~ LAO-TZU

Your living is determined not so much
by what life brings to you as by
the attitude you bring to life; not so much
by what happens to you as by the way
your mind looks at what happens.

~ KAHLIL GIBRAN

The art of knowing is knowing
what to ignore.

~ RUMI

AUGUST 22

In three words
I can sum up everything
I've learned about life:
it goes on.

~ ROBERT FROST

To live is the rarest thing in the world.
Most people exist, that is all.

~ OSCAR WILDE

You pray in your distress and
in your need; would that you might
pray also in the fullness of your joy
and in your days of abundance.

~ KAHLIL GIBRAN

Let go of the battle. Breathe quietly
and let it be. Let your body relax
and your heart soften.

~ JACK KORNFIELD

AUGUST 26

Life goes by fast. Enjoy it.
Calm down. It's all funny.

~ JOAN RIVERS

Most new discoveries
are suddenly-seen
things that were
always there.

~ Susanne K. Langer

AUGUST 28

Some things have to be
believed to be seen.

~ Madeleine L'Engle

AUGUST 29

Don't be pushed by your problems.
Be led by your dreams.

~ RALPH WALDO EMERSON

AUGUST 30

A goal without a plan
is just a wish.

~ ANTOINE DE SAINT-EXUPÉRY

When you consider things
like the stars, our affairs
don't seem to matter very much,
do they?

~ VIRGINIA WOOLF

SEPTEMBER

BALANCE

Life is about balance. The good and the bad.
The highs and the lows. The piña and the colada.

~ Ellen DeGeneres

Learn from yesterday, live for today,
look to tomorrow, rest this afternoon.

~ CHARLES M. SCHULZ

It is perfectly true,
as philosophers say,
that life must be understood
backwards. But they forget
the other proposition,
that it must be lived forwards.

~ SØREN KIERKEGAARD

When we lose one blessing,
another is often most
unexpectedly given in its place.

~ C. S. LEWIS

You must learn to be still
in the midst of activity
and vibrantly alive in repose.

~ INDIRA GANDHI

Lend yourself to others,
but give yourself to yourself.

~ MICHEL DE MONTAIGNE

Now and then it's good
to pause in our pursuit of
happiness and just be happy.

~ GUILLAUME APOLLINAIRE

What is joy without sorrow? What is success
without failure? What is a win without a loss?
What is health without illness?
You have to experience each if you
are to appreciate the other.

~ MARK TWAIN

SEPTEMBER 9

There is no such thing
as work-life balance.
Everything worth fighting
for unbalances your life.

~ ALAIN DE BOTTON

If you are good life is good.

~ Roald Dahl

The art of being wise
is knowing what to overlook.

~ WILLIAM JAMES

All the art of living
lies in a fine mingling
of letting go
and holding on.

~ HAVELOCK ELLIS

Laugh at the things that hurt you
just to keep yourself in balance,
just to keep the world
from running you plumb crazy.

~ KEN KESEY

Don't get so busy making a living
that you forget to make a life.

~ DOLLY PARTON

You are only afraid if you are not
in harmony with yourself.

~ HERMANN HESSE

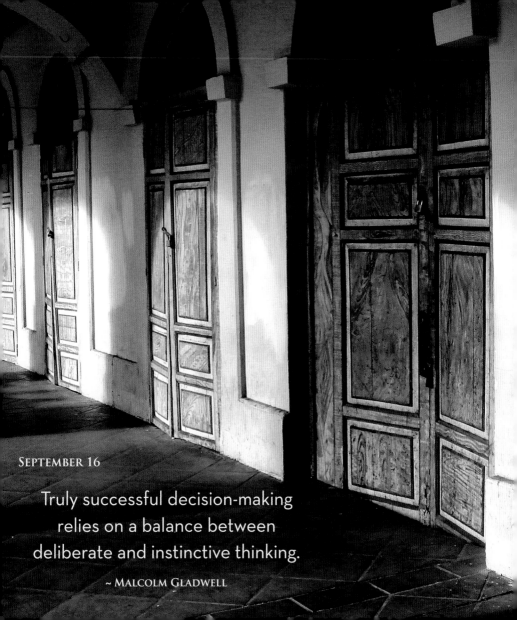

SEPTEMBER 16

Truly successful decision-making
relies on a balance between
deliberate and instinctive thinking.

~ MALCOLM GLADWELL

SEPTEMBER 17

Letting go gives us freedom, and freedom
is the only condition for happiness.

~ THÍCH NHAT HANH

The power is in the balance:
we are our injuries, as much
as we are our successes.

~ BARBARA KINGSOLVER

We have so much time
and so little to do.
Strike that, reverse it.

~ ROALD DAHL

Always aim at complete harmony
of thought and word and deed.

~ MAHATMA GANDHI

The key question to keep asking is,
Are you spending your time
on the right things? Because time
is all you have.

~ RANDY PAUSCH

SEPTEMBER 22

Even a happy life cannot be without
a measure of darkness, and the word
"happy" would lose its meaning
if it were not balanced by sadness.

~ C. G. JUNG

We need to learn how
to want what we have, not to have
what we want in order to get steady
and stable Happiness.

~ DALAI LAMA XIV

SEPTEMBER 24

Besides the noble art
of getting things done,
there is a nobler art
of leaving things undone.
The wisdom of life
consists in the elimination
of nonessentials.

~ LIN YUTANG

Happiness is not a goal;
it's a by-product of a life well lived.

~ ELEANOR ROOSEVELT

Because we all share this planet earth,
we have to learn to live in harmony
and peace with each other and with nature.
This is not just a dream, but a necessity.

~ DALAI LAMA XIV

I do not understand the mystery
of grace—only that it meets us
where we are and does not leave us
where it found us.

~ ANNE LAMOTT

Don't ever confuse the two,
your life and your work.
The second is only a part
of the first.

~ ANNA QUINDLEN

It is not enough
to have great qualities,
we should also have
the management of them.

~ LA ROCHEFOUCAULD

What are you going to do?
Everything, is my guess. It will be a little messy,
but embrace the mess. It will be complicated,
but rejoice in the complications.

~ NORA EPHRON

OCTOBER

TRANQUILLITY

To lie still and think little
is the cheapest medicine
for all diseases of the soul.

~ FRIEDRICH NIETZSCHE

October 2

Nothing can bring you peace
but yourself.

~ Ralph Waldo Emerson

OCTOBER 3

Come from a space of peace
and you'll find that you
can deal with anything.

~ MICHAEL SINGER

Rest and be thankful.

~ WILLIAM WORDSWORTH

All of humanity's
problems stem
from man's inability
to sit quietly
in a room alone.

~ BLAISE PASCAL

Never be in a hurry; do everything quietly
and in a calm spirit. Do not lose
your inner peace for anything whatsoever,
even if your whole world seems upset.

~ ST. FRANCIS DE SALES

Learn to get in touch with the silence
within yourself and know that everything
in this life has a purpose. There are
no mistakes, no coincidences—and all events
are blessings given to us to learn from.

~ ELISABETH KÜBLER-ROSS

Like silence after noise, or cool, clear water
on a hot, stuffy day, Emptiness cleans out
the messy mind and charges up the batteries
of spiritual energy. Many people are afraid
of Emptiness, however, because it
reminds them of Loneliness.

~ BENJAMIN HOFF

OCTOBER 9

Perfect tranquillity within consists
in the good ordering of the mind,
the realm of your own.

~ MARCUS AURELIUS

OCTOBER 10

Inside myself is a place
where I live all alone
and that's where
you renew your springs
that never dry up.

~ PEARL S. BUCK

There is no way to peace;
peace is the way.

~ A. J. MUSTE

With an eye made quiet by the power
of harmony, and the deep power
of joy, we see into the life of things.

~ WILLIAM WORDSWORTH

Silence is more eloquent than words.

~ Thomas Carlyle

Happiness is like a butterfly which,
when pursued, is always beyond
our grasp. But, if you will sit down quietly,
may alight upon you.

~ NATHANIEL HAWTHORNE

OCTOBER 15

True contentment is
the power of getting out
of any situation all
that there is in it.

~ G. K. CHESTERTON

OCTOBER 16

A happy life must be to a great extent
a quiet life—for it is only in an atmosphere
of quiet that true joy can live.

~ BERTRAND RUSSELL

Women need solitude in order to find again
the true essence of themselves.

~ ANNE MORROW LINDBERGH

If something is wrong, fix it if you can.
But train yourself not to worry.
Worry never fixes anything.

~ MARY HEMINGWAY

OCTOBER 19

True silence is the rest of the mind,
and is to the spirit what sleep is to the body:
nourishment and refreshment.

~ WILLIAM PENN

OCTOBER 20

When we are unable to find
tranquillity within ourselves, it is
useless to seek it elsewhere.

~ LA ROCHEFOUCAULD

OCTOBER 21

The Earth has its music
for those who listen.

~ REGINALD VINCENT HOLMES

In the midst of movement and chaos,
keep stillness inside of you.

~ DEEPAK CHOPRA

Don't let the noise of others' opinions
drown out your own inner voice.

~ STEVE JOBS

OCTOBER 24

When words become unclear,
I shall focus with photographs.
When images become inadequate,
I shall be content with silence.

~ ANSEL ADAMS

OCTOBER 25

In order
to understand
the world, one has
to turn away from it
on occasion.

~ ALBERT CAMUS

OCTOBER 26

Go placidly amid the noise
and the haste, and remember
what peace there may be in silence.

~ MAX EHRMANN

I exist as I am. That is enough.

~ WALT WHITMAN

OCTOBER 28

You do not need to leave your room.
Remain sitting at your table and listen. Do not
even listen; simply wait. The world will freely
offer itself to you to be unmasked; it has
no choice. It will roll in ecstasy at your feet.

~ FRANZ KAFKA

Only the development of compassion
and understanding for others can bring us
the tranquillity and happiness we all seek.

~ DALAI LAMA XIV

OCTOBER 30

The greatest thing in the world is
to know how to belong to oneself.

~ MICHEL DE MONTAIGNE

Give up being right. Instead
radiate peace, harmony, love,
and laughter from your heart.

~ DEEPAK CHOPRA

NOVEMBER

KINDNESS

NOVEMBER 1

All great problems demand great love.

~ FRIEDRICH NIETZSCHE

It is the heart always that sees,
before the head can see.

~ THOMAS CARLYLE

The love of our neighbor in all
its fullness simply means being
able to say to him, "What are
you going through?"

~ SIMONE WEIL

NOVEMBER 4

Talk not of wasted affection;
affection was never wasted.

~ HENRY WADSWORTH LONGFELLOW

What draws people to be friends
is that they see the same truth.
They share it.

~ C. S. LEWIS

For small creatures such as we,
the vastness is bearable
only through love.

~ CARL SAGAN

Love and compassion
are necessities,
not luxuries.
Without them, humanity
cannot survive.

~ DALAI LAMA XIV

The only way to speak the truth
is to speak lovingly.

~ HENRY DAVID THOREAU

NOVEMBER 9

The effect of one good-hearted
person is incalculable.

~ ÓSCAR ARIAS SÁNCHEZ

Anything that is of value in life
only multiplies when it is given.

~ DEEPAK CHOPRA

You will learn a lot about yourself
if you stretch in the direction of goodness,
of bigness, of kindness, of forgiveness,
of emotional bravery.

~ CHERYL STRAYED

Always be a little kinder
than necessary.

~ J. M. BARRIE

If I create from the heart,
nearly everything works;
if from the head, almost nothing.

~ MARC CHAGALL

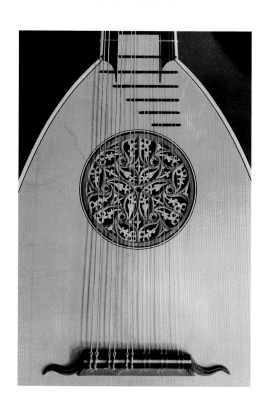

NOVEMBER 14

The ultimate lesson is learning how
to love and be loved unconditionally.

~ ELISABETH KÜBLER-ROSS

NOVEMBER 15

You don't love because:
you love despite; not for the virtues,
but despite the faults.

~ WILLIAM FAULKNER

The smallest act of kindness
is worth more than
the grandest intention.

~ OSCAR WILDE

A good heart is better than all
the heads in the world.

~ EDWARD BULWER-LYTTON

NOVEMBER 18

What is done in love is done well.

~ VINCENT VAN GOGH

NOVEMBER 19

Beauty is a light
in the heart.

~ KAHLIL GIBRAN

This is a deep, permanent human condition,
this need to be loved and to love.

~ ANNIE PROULX

One of the deep secrets of life
is that all that is really worth the doing
is what we do for others.

~ LEWIS CARROLL

Three things in human life are important:
the first is to be kind; the second is
to be kind; and the third is to be kind.

~ HENRY JAMES

Let us love, since that is all
our hearts were made for.

~ ST. THÉRÈSE DE LISIEUX

NOVEMBER 24

The dedicated life is the life
worth living. You must give
with your whole heart.

~ ANNIE DILLARD

NOVEMBER 25

When we love, we always strive to become
better than we are. When we strive to become
better than we are, everything around us
becomes better too.

~ PAULO COELHO

We find greater lightness and ease
in our lives as we increasingly care
for ourselves and other beings.

~ SHARON SALZBERG

The beginning of love
is the will to let those we love
be perfectly themselves—
the resolution not to twist them
to fit our own image.

~ THOMAS MERTON

NOVEMBER 28

Spread love everywhere you go.
Let no one ever come to you
without leaving happier.

~ MOTHER TERESA

NOVEMBER 29

Love yourself and then learn to
extend that love to others
in every encounter.

~ OPRAH WINFREY

The habit of giving only enhances
the desire to give.

~ WALT WHITMAN

DECEMBER

SIMPLICITY

DECEMBER 1

Simplicity is a matter of taste.

~ STEPHEN HAWKING

It is still best to be honest and truthful;
to make the most of what we have;
to be happy with simple pleasures;
and have courage when things go wrong.

~ LAURA INGALLS WILDER

DECEMBER 3

No need to hurry.
No need to sparkle.
No need to be anybody
but oneself.

~ VIRGINIA WOOLF

DECEMBER 4

Not everything needs to be fixed.

~ RANDY PAUSCH

DECEMBER 5

All we have
is all we need.
All we need
is the awareness
of how blessed
we really are.

~ SARAH BAN BREATHNACH

Good friends, good books,
and a sleepy conscience:
this is the ideal life.

~ MARK TWAIN

DECEMBER 7

There must be more to life
than having everything!

~ MAURICE SENDAK

DECEMBER 8

Our life is frittered away by detail.
Simplify, simplify.

~ HENRY DAVID THOREAU

Everything must be made
as simple as possible.
But not simpler.

~ ALBERT EINSTEIN

DECEMBER 10

We already have
everything we need.

~ PEMA CHÖDRÖN

DECEMBER 11

Set wide the window.
Let me drink the day.

~ EDITH WHARTON

The best things in life
aren't things.

~ ART BUCHWALD

There is nothing like staying at home,
for real comfort.

~ JANE AUSTEN

DECEMBER 14

It's the simple things in life
that are the most extraordinary;
only wise men are able
to understand them.

~ PAULO COELHO

December 15

Simplicity is making
the journey of this life
with just baggage enough.

~ Charles Warner

With freedom, books,
flowers, and the moon,
who could not be happy?

~ OSCAR WILDE

DECEMBER 17

Simple is good.

~ JIM HENSON

DECEMBER 18

Sorrow can be alleviated by good sleep,
a bath, and a glass of wine.

~ St. Thomas Aquinas

Live, travel, adventure, bless,
and don't be sorry.

~ JACK KEROUAC

Nothing is more simple than greatness;
indeed, to be simple is to be great.

~ RALPH WALDO EMERSON

It is very simple to be happy,
but it is very difficult to be simple.

~ RABINDRANATH TAGORE

Simple can be harder than complex:
You have to work hard to get
your thinking clean to make it simple.

~ STEVE JOBS

DECEMBER 23

There's never enough time to do
all the nothing you want.

~ BILL WATTERSON

I believe the nicest and sweetest days are not
those on which anything very splendid
or wonderful or exciting happens—but just those
that bring simple little pleasures.

~ L. M. MONTGOMERY

Do justly. Love mercy.
Walk humbly. This is enough.

~ JOHN ADAMS

DECEMBER 26

Not what we have but what we enjoy
constitutes our abundance.

~ EPICURUS

DECEMBER 27

Smile, breathe
and go slowly.

~ THÍCH NHAT HANH

Life is not complex. We are complex.
Life is simple and the simple thing
is the right thing.

~ OSCAR WILDE

A simple life is its own reward.

~ GEORGE SANTAYANA

Life is really simple, but we insist
on making it complicated.

~ CONFUCIUS

DECEMBER 31

Very little is needed to make
a happy life; it is all within yourself
in your way of thinking.

~ MARCUS AURELIUS

CREDITS

CONTRIBUTOR INDEX

Chödrön, Pema
b. 1936
American Tibetan
Buddhist and author

Chopra, Deepak
b. 1947
Indian medical doctor
and spiritual writer

Churchill, Sir Winston
1874–1965
British prime minister

Coelho, Paulo
b. 1947
Brazilian novelist and
lyricist

Confucius
551–479 B.C.
Chinese philosopher
and teacher

D

Dahl, Roald
1916–1990
British novelist, short
story writer, and
screenwriter

Dalai Lama XIV (Lhamo Dondrub)
b. 1935
Tibetan Buddhist head
monk

Darwin, Charles Robert
1809–1882
English naturalist and
scientist

Dass, Ram
b. 1931
American spiritual
teacher and author

DeGeneres, Ellen Lee
b. 1958
American comedian and
television host

Dickinson, Emily
1830–1886
American poet

Didion, Joan
b. 1934
American journalist and
novelist

Dillard, Annie
b. 1945
American poet, essayist,
and literary critic

Dyke, Henry van
1852–1933
American author,
educator, and clergyman

E

Eckhart, Meister
1260–1328
German theologian and
philosopher

Edison, Thomas Alva
1847–1931
American inventor and
businessman

Ehrmann, Max
1872–1945
American writer, poet,
and attorney

Einstein, Albert
1879–1955
German-American
theoretical physicist

Eisenhower, Dwight David
1890–1969
American president

Eliot, George (Mary Anne Evans)
1819–1880
British novelist

Eliot, T. S. (Thomas Stearns)
1888–1965
British poet and
playwright

Ellis, Henry Havelock
1859–1939
British physician, writer,
and social reformer

Emerson, Ralph Waldo
1803–1882
American essayist,
lecturer, and poet

Ephron, Nora
1941–2012
American screenwriter,
producer, and journalist

Epictetus
A.D. 55–135
Greek sage and Stoic
philosopher

Epicurus
341–270 B.C.
Greek philosopher

Erdrich, Louise
b. 1954
Native American writer

F

Faulkner, William
1897–1962
American writer

Fierstein, Harvey
b. 1954
American actor and
playwright

Fink, Sheri
b. 1969
American journalist

Fitzgerald, F. Scott (Francis Scott Key)
1896–1940
American author

Francis de Sales, St.
1567–1622
Bishop of Geneva

Francis of Assisi, St.
1182–1226
Italian Catholic friar
and preacher

Frank, Anne
1929–1945
German diarist

Frost, Robert
1874–1963
American poet

G

Gaiman, Neil Richard MacKinnon
b. 1960
English author

Gandhi, Indira Priyadarshini
1917–1984
Indian prime minister

Gandhi, Mahatma (Mohandas Karamchand)
1869–1948
Indian civil rights
leader

Gawain, Shakti (Carol Louisa)
b. 1948
American author

Gibran, Kahlil
1883–1931
Lebanese-American artist, poet, writer, and philosopher

Gilbert, Elizabeth
b. 1969
American writer

Gladwell, Malcolm
b. 1963
Canadian journalist and author

Goethe, Johann Wolfgang von
1749–1832
German novelist, poet, playwright, and philosopher

Gogh, Vincent van
1853–1890
Dutch artist

Gracián, Baltasar
1601–1658
Spanish Jesuit, writer, and philosopher

Green, John Michael
b. 1977
American author

H

Hammarskjöld, Dag
1905–1961
Swedish diplomat, economist, and author

Hanh, Thích Nhat
b. 1926
Vietnamese Buddhist monk, poet, author, and activist

Hare, Sir David
b. 1947
English playwright, screenwriter, and director

Haskins, Henry Stanley
1875–1957
Stockbroker and man of letters

Hawking, Stephen
b. 1942
English theoretical physicist, cosmologist, and author

Hawthorne, Nathaniel
1804–1864
American novelist

Hazlitt, William
1778–1830
English writer

Heine, Heinrich (Christian Johann)
1797–1856
German poet and journalist

Hemingway, Ernest
1899–1961
American author and journalist

Hemingway, Mary Welsh
1908–1986
American journalist

Henri, Robert
1865–1929
American painter and teacher

Henson, Jim
1936–1990
American puppeteer and creator of the Muppets

Hesse, Hermann
1877–1962
German-Swiss poet, novelist, and painter

Hoff, Benjamin
b. 1946
American author

Holmes, Reginald Vincent
1896–unknown
American poet and author

I

Ishiguro, Kazuo
b. 1954
Japanese-born British novelist

J

James, Henry
1843–1916
English writer

James, William
1842–1910
American psychologist and philosopher

Jameson, Storm (Margaret)
1891–1986
English journalist and author

Jobs, Steve (Steven Paul)
1955–2011
American entrepreneur and co-founder of Apple Inc.

Joyce, James
1882–1941
Irish novelist and poet

Jung, C. G. (Carl Gustav)
1875–1961
Swiss psychiatrist and founder of analytical psychology

K

Kafka, Franz
1883–1924
Austro-Hungarian novelist

Kenmore, Carolyn
b. 1949
American model and author

Kerouac, Jack
1922–1969
American novelist and poet

Kesey, Kenneth Elton
1935–2001
American author

Kessler, David
b. 1959
American author and public speaker

Kierkegaard, Søren
1813–1855
Danish philosopher, theologian, and writer

King, Coretta Scott
1927–2006
American author, activist, and civil rights leader

King, Martin Luther, Jr.
1929–1968
American clergyman, activist, and civil rights leader

King, Stephen
b. 1947
American novelist

Kingsolver, Barbara
b. 1955
American novelist, poet, and essayist

Kornfield, Jack
b. 1945
American author and teacher

Krakauer, Jon
b. 1954
American writer

Kübler-Ross, Elisabeth
1926–2004
American psychiatrist and author

L

Lamott, Anne
b. 1954
American novelist and nonfiction writer

Landers, Ann (Eppie Lederer)
1918–2002
American advice columnist

Langer, Susanne Katherina
1895–1985
American philosopher and writer

Lao-tzu
604–531 B.C.
Chinese philosopher

Le Guin, Ursula K.
b. 1929
American novelist, poet, and essayist

L'Engle, Madeleine
1918–2007
American writer

Lewis, C. S. (Clive Staples)
1898–1963
British novelist, essayist, and theologian

Lindbergh, Anne Morrow
1906–2001
American writer, poet, and aviator

Longfellow, Henry Wadsworth
1807–1882
American poet

M

Maeterlinck, Maurice (Polydore Marie Bernard)
1862–1949
Belgian playwright, poet, and essayist

Mandela, Nelson
1918–2013
South African president

Meredith, George
1828–1909
English novelist and poet

Merton, Thomas
1915–1968
American writer

Miller, Henry
1891–1980
American novelist

Milne, A. A. (Alan Alexander)
1882–1956
English novelist, poet, and playwright

Montaigne, Michel de
1533–1592
French writer and philosopher

Montgomery, L. M. (Lucy Maud)
1874–1942
Canadian novelist

Morrison, Toni (Chloe Ardelia Wofford)
b. 1931
American novelist and poet

Mumford, Lewis
1895–1990
American historian, philosopher, and literary critic

Munro, Alice
b. 1931
Canadian author

Murakami, Haruki
b. 1949
Japanese writer

Muste, A. J. (Abraham Johannes)
1885–1967
Dutch-born American clergyman and political activist

N

Narihira, Ariwara no
A.D. 825–880
Japanese waka poet and aristocrat

Niebuhr, Reinhold (Karl Paul)
1892–1971
American theologian and professor

Nietzsche, Friedrich
1844–1900
German philosopher and poet

Nightingale, Florence
1820–1910
English social reformer and founder of modern nursing philosophy

Nin, Anaïs
1903–1977
French diarist and novelist

Nixon, Richard Milhous
1913–1994
American president

O

Ovid (Publius Ovidius Naso)
43 B.C.–A.D. 17
Roman poet

P

Parton, Dolly
b. 1946
American singer-songwriter

Pascal, Blaise
1623–1662
French mathematician, philosopher, and writer

Patrick, Simon
1626–1707
English theologian and bishop

Pausch, Randy (Randolph Frederick)
1960–2008
American professor

Penn, William
1644–1718
English philosopher

Perry, Tyler
b. 1969
American actor and author

Phillpotts, Eden
1862–1960
English author, poet, and dramatist

Plato
428–348 B.C.
Ancient Greek philosopher

Plutarch
A.D. 46–120
Greek historian

Poehler, Amy Meredith
b. 1971
American actress, comedian, and author

Prince (Prince Rogers Nelson)
b. 1958
American singer-songwriter and actor

Proulx, Annie (Edna)
b. 1935
American journalist and author

Proust, Marcel
1871–1922
French novelist

Q

Quindlen, Anna
b. 1952
American journalist and novelist

R

Reeve, Christopher D'Olier
1952–2004
American actor, author, and activist

Reiner, Rob (Robert)
b. 1947
American actor, director, and activist

Rilke, Rainer Maria
1875–1926
Bohemian Austrian poet

Rivers, Joan (Alexandra Molinsky)
1933-2014
American actress, comedian, writer, and producer

Rochefoucauld, François VI, Duc de La
1613–1680
French author

Rockefeller, John Davison
1839–1937
American business magnate and philanthropist

Rogers, Frederick McFeely
1928–2003
American educator and television personality

Roosevelt, (Anna) Eleanor
1884–1962
American first lady, activist, and author

Rowling, J. K. (Joanne Kathleen)
b. 1965
British novelist

Roy, Arundhati (Suzanna)
b. 1961
Indian author and political activist

Rudolph, Wilma Glodean
1940–1994
American athlete and Olympic champion

Rukeyser, Muriel
1913–1980
American poet and political activist

Rumi (Jalal ad-Din Muhammad Rumi)
1207–1273
Persian poet

Russell, Bertrand
1872–1970
British philosopher, mathematician, and social critic

S

Sagan, Carl
1934–1996
American astronomer, astrophysicist, and author

Saint-Exupéry, Antoine de
1900–1944
French writer, poet, and aviator

Salzberg, Sharon
b. 1952
American author and teacher

Sánchez, Óscar Arias
b. 1940
Costa Rican president

Santayana, George
1863–1952
Spanish-American philosopher, essayist, poet, and novelist

Saroyan, William
1908–1981
Armenian-American dramatist and author

Sartre, Jean-Paul
1905–1980
French philosopher, playwright, and novelist

Schulz, Charles Monroe
1922–2000
American cartoonist

Sendak, Maurice Bernard
1928–2012
American illustrator and writer

Shaw, George Bernard
1856–1950
Irish playwright

Singer, Michael
b. 1947
American author

Steinbeck, John
1902–1968
American novelist

Stevenson, Robert Louis
1850–1894
Scottish novelist, poet, and writer

Stockett, Kathryn
b. 1969
American novelist

Strayed, Cheryl
b. 1968
American author

T

Tagore, Rabindranath
1861–1941
Bengali poet, novelist, essayist, and composer

Teresa, Mother (Agnes Gonxha Bojaxhiu)
1910–1997
Albanian-Indian nun and religious leader

Thérèse de Lisieux, St.
1873–1897
French Carmelite nun

Thiruvalluvar
unknown
Tamil poet and philosopher

Thomas Aquinas, St.
1225–1274
Italian priest, philosopher, and theologian

Thoreau, Henry David
1817–1862
American author, poet, and philosopher

Tolkien, J.R.R. (John Ronald Reuel)
1892–1973
English writer, poet, and professor

Tolle, Eckhart
b. 1948
German spiritual teacher and writer

Tutu, Desmond
b. 1931
South African religious leader and antiapartheid activist

Twain, Mark (Samuel Langhorne Clemens)
1835–1910
American novelist and humorist

Tzu, Sun
544–496 B.C.
Chinese military general, strategist, and philosopher

V

Vanzant, Iyanla
b. 1953
American author and speaker

Vauvenargues, Luc de Clapiers, marquis de
1715–1747
French writer and moralist

Vonnegut, Kurt
1922–2007
American writer

W

Walker, Alice
b. 1944
American novelist, poet, and activist

Wallace, David Foster
1962–2008
American author and professor

Warner, Charles Dudley
1829–1900
American essayist and novelist

Washington, George
1732–1799
American president

Watterson, Bill (William Boyd II)
b. 1958
American cartoonist and author

Weil, Simone
1909–1943
French philosopher and political activist

Wesley, John
1703–1791
Anglican evangelist and founder of the Wesleyan Tradition

Wharton, Edith Newbold Jones
1862–1937
American novelist

White, E. B. (Elwyn Brooks)
1899–1985
American writer

Whitman, Walt
1819–1892
American poet, essayist, and journalist

Wilde, Oscar
1854–1900
Irish novelist and dramatist

Wilder, Laura Ingalls
1867–1957
American author

Wilder, Thornton
1897–1975
American playwright and novelist

Williams, Sir Bernard Arthur Owen
1929–2003
English philosopher and author

Williamson, Marianne
b. 1952
American author and speaker

Winfrey, Oprah
b. 1954
American media personality

Woolf, Virginia (Adeline)
1882–1941
British novelist and essayist

Woollcott, Alexander
1887–1943
American critic and journalist

Wordsworth, William
1770–1850
English poet

Wright, Frank Lloyd
1867–1959
American architect

Y

Yousafzai, Malala
b. 1997
Pakistani activist and Nobel Prize recipient

Yutang, Lin
1895–1976
Chinese novelist, essayist, and translator

ILLUSTRATIONS CREDITS

JANUARY

Opener, Tomas Tichy/Shutterstock; 1, Andrea Obzerova/Shutterstock; 2, SOPA RF/SOPA/Corbis; 3, Kerstin Hinze/naturepl.com; 4, bojabo/iStockphoto; 5, Yatra/Shutterstock; 6, Shannon Hibberd/National Geographic Creative; 7, Clint Spencer/iStockphoto; 8, Brian A. Jackson/Shutterstock; 9, Shikhei Goh/National Geographic Your Shot; 10, gjp311/iStockphoto; 11, KerstinIvarsson/iStockphoto; 12, Nekan/iStockphoto; 13, Crepesoles/Shutterstock; 14, viki2win/Shutterstock; 15, Peter Mukherjee/iStockphoto; 16, Cateye777/iStockphoto; 17, Sandra Marsh/National Geographic Your Shot; 18, ESA and NASA; 19, Roy McMahon/Corbis; 20, Jason Rydquist/National Geographic Your Shot; 21, ehrlif/iStockphoto; 22, Wilm Ihlenfeld/Shutterstock; 23, Louie Psihoyos/CORBIS; 24, blackwaterimages/iStockphoto; 25, Irina Rogova/Shutterstock; 26, Thomas Bethge/Shutterstock; 27, MarioGuti/iStockphoto; 28, Carl R. Battreall/Design Pics Inc/National Geographic Creative; 29, Firefly Productions/Corbis; 30, Kathrine Lloyd/National Geographic Your Shot; 31, mikkelwilliam/iStockphoto.

FEBRUARY

Opener, Magone/iStockphoto; 1, Manjunath Undi/National Geographic Your Shot; 2, John Munro/National Geographic Your Shot; 3, Doug Meek/Corbis; 4, Jose Yee/National Geographic Your Shot; 5, heibaihui/iStockphoto; 6, EM Arts/Shutterstock; 7, Givaga/iStockphoto; 8, Africa Studio/Shutterstock; 9, SumikoPhoto/iStockphoto; 10, Tommy Eliassen/National Geographic Your Shot; 11, tvirbickis/iStockphoto; 12, Tom Soucek/Design Pics Inc/National Geographic Creative; 13, Rrrainbow/Shutterstock; 14, Marketa Pavleye/Offset; 15, imagevillage/iStockphoto; 16, Michael Hero/Shutterstock; 17, stevemart/Shutterstock; 18, Jane Sheng/National Geographic

Your Shot; 19, flybyphi2001/iStockphoto; 20, littlesam/Shutterstock; 21, Patricio Robles Gil/Sierra Madre/Minden Pictures; 22, Matthew George/National Geographic Your Shot; 23, spxChrome/iStockphoto; 24, Hardi Budi/National Geographic Your Shot; 25, susabell/iStockphoto; 26, Tracing Tea/Shutterstock; 27, Patrick J. Endres/AlaskaPhotoGraphics/Corbis; 28/29, f9photos/iStockphoto.

MARCH

Opener, Guoqiang Xue/Shutterstock; 1, Craig Lee/San Francisco Chronicle/Corbis; 2, Razvan/iStockphoto; 3, da-kuk/iStockphoto; 4, kojihirano/Shutterstock; 5, Scorpp/Shutterstock; 6, Rike/iStockphoto; 7, Nemeziya/Shutterstock; 8, pavrich/iStockphoto; 9, Anton Jankovoy/National Geographic Creative/Corbis; 10, pilipphoto/iStockphoto; 11, jakubzak/iStockphoto; 12, Scacciamosche/iStockphoto; 13, tanewpix/Shutterstock; 14, Sam Diephuis/Corbis; 15, Doug Perrine/naturepl.com; 16, colevineyard/iStockphoto; 17, Kyslynskyy/iStockphoto; 18, Rados/Shutterstock; 19, GeniusKp/Shutterstock; 20, Pinkyone/Shutterstock; 21, Tomas Tichy/Shutterstock; 22, dangdumrong/iStockphoto; 23, Ivan Nakonechnyy/Shutterstock; 24, Daniel Kuhne/National Geographic Your Shot; 25, Mario Aguilar/National Geographic Your Shot; 26, Ian Egner/Robert Harding World Imagery/Corbis; 27, macbrianmun/iStockphoto; 28, Vold77/iStockphoto; 29, Jeff Stenstrom/National Geographic Your Shot; 30, lola1960/iStockphoto; 31, Igor Normann/Shutterstock.

APRIL

Opener, Tina Thuell/National Geographic Your Shot; 1, wingmar/iStockphoto; 2, Edwin Giesbers/naturepl.com; 3, Dan Sheehan/Science Faction/Corbis; 4, ultramarinfoto/iStockphoto; 5, Floortje/iStockphoto; 6, Love Silhouette/Shutterstock; 7, fotoclick/iStockphoto; 8, Andreea Ionascu/Shutterstock; 9, Georgianna Lane/Garden Photo World/Corbis; 10, Jana Mänz/Westend61/Corbis; 11, Lynne Nicholson/Shutterstock; 12, JaroPienza/Shutterstock; 13, Shannon Hibberd/National Geographic Creative; 14, Tom Murphy/National Geographic Creative; 15, 167/Ralph Lee Hopkins/Ocean/Corbis; 16, Sacco & Watt/Galeries/Corbis; 17, JeniFoto/

DAILY PEACE

Published by the National Geographic Society

Gary E. Knell, *President and Chief Executive Officer*

John M. Fahey, *Chairman of the Board*

Declan Moore, *Chief Media Officer*

Chris Johns, *Chief Content Officer*

Prepared by the Book Division

Hector Sierra, *Senior Vice President and General Manager*

Lisa Thomas, *Senior Vice President and Editorial Director*

Jonathan Halling, *Creative Director*

Marianne R. Koszorus, *Design Director*

Hilary Black, *Senior Editor*

R. Gary Colbert, *Production Director*

Jennifer A. Thornton, *Director of Managing Editorial*

Susan S. Blair, *Director of Photography*

Meredith C. Wilcox, *Director, Administration and Rights Clearance*

Staff for This Book

Allyson Dickman, *Associate Editor*

Melissa Farris, *Art Director*

Katie Olsen, *Designer*

Shannon Hibberd, *Illustrations Editor*

Lindsay Anderson, *Researcher*

Kris Heitkamp, *Assistant Researcher*

Marshall Kiker, *Associate Managing Editor*

Judith Klein, *Senior Production Editor*

Lisa A. Walker, *Production Manager*

Nicole Miller, *Design Production Assistant*

George Bounelis, *Manager, Production Services*

Wendy Smith, *Imaging*